FAMOUS FRIENDS
True Tales of Friendship

Ella FITZGERALD and Marilyn MONROE

Tamra B. Orr

PURPLE TOAD
PUBLISHING

Printing   1   2   3   4   5   6   7   8   9

Babe Ruth and Lou Gehrig
Helen Keller and Mark Twain
Henry Ford and Thomas Edison
Ella Fitzgerald and Marilyn Monroe
Maya Angelou and Oprah Winfrey

Library of Congress Cataloging-in-Publication Data
  Orr, Tamra B.
    Ella Fitzgerald and Marilyn Monroe / Written by: Tamra B. Orr
p. cm.
Includes bibliographic references, glossary, and index.
ISBN 9781624695087
  1. Ella Fitzgerald, 1917 - 1996 — Juvenile literature. 2. Marilyn Monroe, 1926 - 1962 — Juvenile literature. 3. Jazz musicians — United States — Biography — Juvenile literature. 4. Singers — United States — Biography — Juvenile literature. 5. Motion picture actors and actresses — United States — Biography — Juvenile literature. I. Series: Famous Friends – True Tales of Friendship
ML3930.F5 K57 2019
782.42165 B
  [B]

eBook ISBN: 9781624695070

Library of Congress Control Number: 2019942502

ABOUT THE AUTHOR: Tamra B. Orr is a full-time author living in the Pacific Northwest with her family. She graduated from Ball State University in Muncie, Indiana. She has written more than 500 books about everything from historical events and career choices to controversial issues and celebrity biographies. On those rare occasions that she is not writing a book, she is reading one.

PUBLISHER'S NOTE: This story has not been authorized by the estates of Ella Fitzgerald or Marilyn Monroe.

CONTENTS

NORMAN GRANZ' **JAZZ** at the **Philharmonic**

ELLA FITZGERALD
GENE KRUPA QUARTET
THE MODERN JAZZ QUARTET
OSCAR PETERSON TRIO · JO JONES
STAN GETZ · DIZZY GILLESPIE
ROY ELDRIDGE · ILLINOIS JACQUET
FLIP PHILLIPS · SONNY STITT
EDDIE SHU · JOHN LEWIS · MILT JACKSON

Wed. Eve. Sept. 19

CLEVELAND MUSIC HALL, 8:30 P. M.

In the 1940s, Las Vegas hotels and casinos would allow black artists to perform, but not come through the front door or stay to eat or gamble. Norman Granz (above) refused to allow this continued segregation.

CHAPTER 1

"A Real Debt"

He knew exactly what it felt like to be targeted because of his background. Norman Granz was born to immigrant parents and, as a child, had felt the sting of racial slurs and comments. He had also witnessed African Americans being insulted and injured while he served in World War II. He could no longer stand by and watch it happen: he was determined to change things.

And he did—through music.

In 1944, Granz started a concert series called Jazz at the Philharmonic. The majority of his musicians were African American. Whenever he and his performers agreed to appear in any venue, his contracts stated that everyone would be given equal pay, travel, and accommodations. In other words, his black musicians were to be paid the same amount, provided with the same transportation, and given the same hotel rooms as white performers.

This did not go over well with some of the nightclub owners. Even though the owners had agreed to Granz's contracts, the performers were often let into the nightclub only through a back or side door.

Ella Fitzgerald was not always considered glamorous enough to appear in some venues.

They struggled to get rooms in some hotels. At one performance in Texas, the police showed up at the venue and burst into the players' dressing room. They were arrested and taken to the station. Then, in a moment of real irony, a few of the officers asked for the autographs of some of the better-known musicians.

One performer who worked with Granz was young Ella Fitzgerald. Like many up-and-coming music artists, one of the places she most wanted to appear was at the Mocambo, a popular nightclub in West Hollywood.

However, African Americans were not typically welcome there and, if they were, they were definitely not allowed to come through the front door. Although black singers Eartha Kitt and Dorothy Dandridge had performed in the nightclub, owner Charlie Morrison did not feel that Ella Fitzgerald was "glamorous" enough for his stage.

One of the movie stars who came to the Mocambo was Marilyn Monroe. Wherever she went, the

The neon sign at the Mocambo let everyone know who was going to be on the stage.

press was sure to follow, snapping photos and asking questions of the "blonde bombshell," as she was known. When Marilyn heard that Ella Fitzgerald was not allowed to perform at the Mocambo, she knew she had to step in and use her fame for a good cause.

Marilyn had been a fan of Ella Fitzgerald's music for years and often listened to her records. She had seen Ella perform in Los Angeles in November 1954. In early 1955, when she heard how Fitzgerald had been treated, she called Morrison and made him an offer.

Marilyn Monroe may have been glamorous, but she took her acting seriously.

In August 1972, Ella did an interview with *Ms.* magazine and explained what Marilyn did for her. "I owe Marilyn Monroe a real debt," she explained. "She personally called the owner of the Mocambo, and told him she wanted me booked immediately, and if he would do it, she would take a front table every night. She told him—and it was true, due to Marilyn's superstar status—that the press would go wild." Ella continued, "The owner said yes, and Marilyn was there, front table, every night. The press went overboard. After that, I never had to play a small jazz club again. She was an unusual woman—a little ahead of her times. And she didn't know it."[1]

Ella appeared at the Mocambo for two weeks straight—and each night, the shows were sold out. When the weeks ended, Morrison booked her for an additional week. As promised, each night, Marilyn was right there at the front table. The press came and wrote about Ella's amazing performances, and from that point forward, she never had to worry about not being allowed into the biggest nightclubs.

She did not even worry about which door she would come through, as Marilyn also made sure that was not a problem. As Geoffrey Mark, author of a biography about Ella, stated to *Fox News*, Marilyn followed Ella around to her many concerts. Whenever she saw that she was only allowed through a side door, he said, "She would go to management and say, 'If Ella doesn't go through the front door, I won't either. And she would grab Ella's arm and together they went in."[2]

After her performance at the Mocambo, Fitzgerald performed at a club in Colorado that refused to let her enter through the front door. Monroe showed up to complain to the owners, and this treatment was stopped, both there and at other clubs.

As the two women got to know each other, Ella and Marilyn realized they had far more in common than just a love of jazz music. They both had survived traumatic childhoods—and they were still struggling. Although their friendship lasted barely eight years, it was one that impacted them both greatly.

Half a century ago, walking down the Sunset Strip at night in West Hollywood, California, was awe-inspiring. The darkness was beaten back by the glitter and glare of lights coming from nightclubs such as Café Trocadero, Ciro's, and the Mocambo. The street was full of sound as all types of music spilled out the front doors of each club and down the sidewalks. This is where the celebrities spent their weekends, dressing up, sliding into booths and up to tables, and listening to the latest hot singer, from Frank Sinatra to Ella Fitzgerald.

When the Mocambo opened in early 1941, its Mexico-themed design cost today's equivalent of $1.6 million to decorate. It had glass-walled cages of macaws, cockatoos, and other parrots. Outside, a huge marquee displayed the name of who was performing that night, beckoning customers with bright lights and neon. For more than 15 years, the Mocambo was the place to be. It truly was *the* "playground to the stars."

Ciro's was one of the more popular nightclubs in West Hollywood during the 1940s.

Marilyn is followed by photographers as she arrives at Ciro's nightclub in 1953. Above: The one-year-old Marilyn in 1927.

The Difficult Life of the "Blonde Bombshell"

From the moment Norma Jean Mortenson was born on June 1, 1926, in Los Angeles, California, she had a difficult life. She never knew her father and was not even sure who he was. When she was baptized, her name became Norma Jean (or Jeane) Baker. Her mother, Gladys Monroe Baker, suffered from severe mental illness and was either absent or abusive. By the time Norma Jean reached her teens, she had been in more than a dozen foster homes and had suffered physical and sexual abuse. She had a half-sister whom she barely knew. "There was always dry bread, the army cot by the water heater, the monthly visit from the county social worker who inspected the soles of her shoes and patted the top of her head and went away," described a *Time* feature article on Marilyn from 1956.[1] At 15, Norma Jean dropped out of Van Nuys High School. She needed an escape, a way to rise above her painful childhood—and she found it in the boy who lived next door.

His name was Jimmy Dougherty, and he was four years older than 16-year-old Norma Jean. He proposed and she said yes, hoping it

During World War II, Marilyn worked at a local munitions factory.

would take her life in a new direction. The two were married on June 19, 1942. Not long after the wedding, Dougherty, a merchant marine, was shipped off to the South Pacific to fight in World War II. While he was overseas, Norma Jean began working at the Radio Plane Munitions Factory in Burbank, California. She started as a parachute inspector, and then shifted to paint sprayer.

One day a photographer named David Conover came to the factory to take some pictures for *Yank* magazine. He was writing a story about how women were contributing to the war effort by taking jobs traditionally held by men. He saw Norma Jean and immediately recognized a potential model. Conover spoke with her and began sending her modeling jobs. She took a three-month modeling course. Within two years, Norma Jean was appearing on magazine covers often—and she was ready to reach for her dream to become an actress.

By the time Dougherty returned to the United States, his wife had a modeling career, had dyed her hair blonde, and had changed her name to Marilyn Monroe. The two divorced in 1946, and soon after, Marilyn had her first movie contract. At first she was given only small

Monroe appeared in acclaimed director John Huston's *Asphalt Jungle*, a film about a jewel robbery that goes wrong. The film was so successful, it later became a television series.

roles. However, in 1950, she appeared in *The Asphalt Jungle*. This movie brought her so much attention from the media and the fans that she was cast in a bigger role in *All about Eve*.

From that moment forward, Marilyn became known the world over. As she appeared in more and more movies, she also popped up in hundreds of stories in magazines and newspapers. Photographs of her were everywhere. Marilyn was not only talented, she was model-beautiful. She knew how to move, speak, and behave to thrill her audiences. She could act, sing, and dance, and do it all with a sense of humor. Soon she was receiving more than 5,000 fan letters a week, a lot of them from soldiers who sent marriage proposals.

Tony Curtis and Marilyn Monroe simmer in Billy Wilder's *Some Like It Hot*, considered one of Hollywood's greatest comedies.

Many of Marilyn's movies were comedies, including *Gentlemen Prefer Blondes* and *Some Like It Hot*. Others were more serious dramas, such as *Niagara* and *Bus Stop*. Almost all of them were huge hits, and Marilyn earned several Golden Globe Awards for her acting.

Marilyn's personal life was watched closely too. On January 14, 1954, she married baseball legend Joe DiMaggio. The two were married for only nine months, however. The Yankees slugger struggled with how much attention his wife got from male fans. The two were divorced by the end of the year. Less than two years later, Marilyn married for the third time, to prizewinning playwright Arthur Miller. They were married for four and a half years before getting divorced on January 20, 1961.

Although Marilyn was considered one of the most beautiful and successful actors in the world, her life was full of challenges. She often suffered from anxiety, getting so nervous before a public appearance that she'd feel sick

America was entranced by the marriage of Marilyn Monroe and Joe DiMaggio.

and arrive late. Sometimes she even broke out in hives from nerves. By the mid-1950s, she was weary of playing the "dumb blonde" in movies. She backed out of a movie contract and moved to New York City to take acting classes. She only wanted to take roles that were more serious and dramatic. She formed her own production company and performed in *Bus Stop* and *The Prince and Showgirl*.

In addition to dealing with anxiety, Marilyn's divorces and the miscarriages she had experienced drove her to drinking a great deal of alcohol and taking pills. She was often depressed and struggling emotionally. In *The Unfinished Biography of Marilyn Monroe*, she stated, "I knew I belonged to the public and to the world, not because I was talented or even beautiful but because I had never belonged to anything or anyone else."[2]

In 1961, Marilyn's last complete movie, *The Misfits*, was released.

Lee Strasberg, director of the famed Actors Studio, taught method acting, and in 1955, he became Monroe's tutor. She amazed her classmates with serious acting she'd seldom been able to show onscreen. Strasberg later said two of the greatest acting talents he worked with were Marlon Brando and Marilyn Monroe.

In *The Misfits*, Monroe's final film, she teamed up again with director John Huston and costarred with Clark Gable (right). It would also be Gable's last film. The story was written by her playwright ex-husband, Arthur Miller.

She was slated to film *Something's Got to Give* next, but she missed so many days on set that she was eventually fired. On May 19, 1962, the actor made history by singing a very steamy "Happy Birthday" to President John F. Kennedy, spurring rumors that the two of them were in a secret romantic relationship. Less than three months later, 36-year-old Marilyn was found dead in her bedroom, an empty bottle of sleeping pills next to her. Her death was ruled a suicide. No note was left behind.

The world mourned the beloved actress that had entertained audiences in 29 films, countless newspaper and magazine articles, photographs, and television reports. In the end, perhaps Norma Jean had not been able to find the escape she had hoped for—but she certainly made the world a brighter place while she was here.

A New Look at
Marilyn and Ella

In 2003, American-British writer Bonnie Greer happened to catch a documentary on the Biography Channel about the life of Marilyn Monroe and her friendship with Ella Fitzgerald. "I was shocked," Greer told *The Independent*. "It was all of a second and immediately I visualised Ella Fitzgerald and Marilyn Monroe, an unlikely pairing." Greer decided to write a play about the two women. She said that she was inspired, in great part, by the differences between Ella and Marilyn's looks. "One of the things that's important to me is to have a black woman who is not conventionally beautiful worshipped by one of the most beautiful women in the world who can see her inner quality."

Greer's play, *Marilyn and Ella* was a hit in England. It appealed to fans of the two women, but it also educated them. "Most people look at the photograph [on the front of the program] and say, 'That's a really clever idea, putting Marilyn and Ella together,' and we say, 'no, it's a true story,' " stated the play's producer, Colin McFarlane.[3]

Bonnie Greer's play Marilyn and Ella was performed at the Theatre Royal Stratford East in 2008 and later at the Apollo Theatre, in London's West End.

17

When Fitzgerald took the stage, even jazz greats like
Dizzy Gillespie (right) were fascinated by her voice.

"The First Lady of Song"

It was a last-minute decision that changed the entire course of her life. On November 21, 1934, fifteen-year-old Ella Fitzgerald was a contestant in the Apollo Theater's Amateur Night, thanks to a bet she had made with some friends. She did not look like a contestant. She wore torn clothes and men's boots. She was living on the streets, but she had been practicing her dance moves for weeks. As she waited to go on stage, she realized that the act ahead of her, the local dance duo, the Edwards Sisters, was thrilling the audience. Applause roared through the theater. Suddenly Ella was not sure if she wanted to try to follow an act that popular.

As she walked out into the spotlight, Ella made a sudden decision. Instead of dancing, she would sing. She loved to sing and knew a number of songs by heart, especially those by a current singer named Connee Boswell. "My mother brought home one of her records, and I fell in love with it," Ella recalled in a later interview. "I tried so hard to sound just like her."[1] The teenager launched into "The Object of My Affection" and followed it up with

The Apollo Theater was the starting point for many African American performers and continues to be so.

"Judy." The audience was absolutely amazed. Ella came in first in that night's contest, winning $25. However, she was not allowed to claim the additional prize of a paid appearance at the Apollo. She simply did not have the clothing or the looks for it. Despite being back on the streets, Ella knew that from this point forward, she was not a dancer. Instead, she was a singer. And she was right. One day, she would be known as "the first lady of song."

Ella Fitzgerald was born April 25, 1917, in Newport News, Virginia. Her parents, William Fitzgerald and Temperance Williams, separated while Ella was still a baby. A good student, Ella did well until she was a young teen, when her mother was killed in a car accident. Then, her life changed dramatically. Temperance's boyfriend began abusing Ella, and she was taken in by an aunt. Soon, Ella quit high school and ran away from home. She was caught and sent to a reformatory school. Geoffrey Mark, author of a biography of Ella, wrote, "It was an unfortunate set of circumstances . . . because she ran away, the government grabbed her and stuck her in this awful place where children were sent—far away from where she was living."[2]

Ella spent a year at the school. It was so awful there that, even as an adult, she rarely spoke of that time in her life. As one of the few African American students there, she was kept in a segregated area. Daily beatings were common. Despite the horrible treatment she received, Ella did not give up. As Mark stated, "She believed that if she did the right thing, if she worked hard, the outcome would come out in her favor."[3]

Six months after her performance at the Apollo, Ella was approached by Chick Webb, a band leader. He wanted to sign her. "I thought my singing was pretty much hollering, but Webb didn't," Ella said later.[4] In 1935, Ella recorded her first song, "Love and Kisses." She followed it with a novelty song based on a nursery rhyme, "A-Tisket, A-Tasket." The song quickly became popular and made young Ella a star. Over the next seven years, she recorded more than 150 songs.

Ella was very humble, never believing that she was that talented.

When Ella signed with agent Norman Granz to tour across the country, she began expanding the type of songs she sang. "I had gotten to the point where I was only singing be-bop," she stated. "Norman came along, and he felt that I should do other things. . . . [It] was a turning point in my life."[5] She branched out to perform with small jazz groups and big bands, singing everything from show tunes and jazz to opera and gospel. She sang alone, in duets, and with groups like the Ink Spots. She even mastered the art of scatting, adding it to many of her songs.

Ella appeared on a number of television variety and talk shows and recorded with some of the biggest names in jazz, including Duke

During Ella's many concerts, it was clear that she could perform almost any kind of music.

Many of Ella's songs were performed with other artists, including trumpet player and singer Louis Armstrong.

Ellington, Count Basie, and Louis Armstrong. Standing in front of thousands in venues like Carnegie Hall, it was hard to imagine that this was the same woman who thought of herself as shy. "I'm very shy, and I shy away from people," she admitted in an interview. "But the moment I hit the stage, it's a different feeling. I get nerve from somewhere; maybe it's because it's something I love to do."[6]

As a young woman, Ella had married a shipyard worker named Benjamin Kornegay. When she discovered that he was also a criminal, she had the marriage annulled. In 1947, she married musician Ray Brown. The two of them adopted the son of Ella's half-sister Frances and named him Ray, Jr. This marriage ended in 1953.

By the late 1950s, Ella was everywhere—from *The Ed Sullivan Show* and Carnegie Hall to international concerts and—thanks to Marilyn—Hollywood's Mocambo. She was touring 40 to 45 weeks out of the year—and exhaustion was taking a toll on her and her health. In 1965, she almost collapsed while on stage in Munich. In 1967, she was given the Recording Academy's Lifetime Achievement Award. In 1972, she and Carol Channing performed the half-time show during Super Bowl VI.

During the 1960s, Ella spent much of her time on the road, traveling from one performance to another, often with other jazz legends such as Oscar Peterson (left).

With such a demanding schedule, it did not take long for Ella to show the signs of tiring.

The two did a tribute to Louis Armstrong, and Ella became the first African American woman to perform during this huge sports event.

In the 1970s, Ella was diagnosed with diabetes, and in 1986, she underwent quintuple bypass heart surgery. She returned to the spotlight in 1987, determined to keep performing. That year, President Ronald Reagan gave her the National Medal of Arts. Even though she had to be helped to and from the stage, she still managed to wow the crowd after receiving the medal, singing "You are the Sunshine of My Life." It included the scatting that she was known for. She received a standing ovation.

Ella's last concert was in 1991 at Carnegie Hall. When she was asked what it felt like to be a legend, Ella responded, "I don't think I noticed it at first." She stated that by the mid-1950s, however, "it just seemed that more people began to like my singing. The awards I started winning didn't make me feel important, but they made me realize people loved me. And then kids started calling me 'Ella'—half of them never even mentioned 'Ella Fitzgerald'—just 'Ella.' "[7]

In 1993, due to complications from her diabetes, Ella underwent surgery to amputate both of her legs below her knees. She never fully recovered from the operation. She died on June 15, 1996, at the age of 79. During her life, she recorded more than 200 albums and 2,000 songs.

In 1987, President Ronald Reagan gave Ella the National Medal of Arts for her years of bringing music and joy to people's lives.

The Story of Scatting

What is scatting? Mostly it is a musical blend of nonsense words made up of rhythmic syllables such as *doo-yah-dah-dit-dip-bah!* Scatting is as much a part of jazz music as trombones—but how did it get started? One legend gives credit to jazz great Louis Armstrong. In 1926, as he recorded the song "Heebie Jeebies," he apparently forgot the lyrics, so he improvised with what some call "vocal hokum." The style caught on and was imitated by many different musicians. Ella Fitzgerald used it and quickly became one of the very best.

While some may have believed scatting was just done for fun, it actually allowed musicians to get creative, to escape standard lyrics, and to use their voice like a musical instrument. Today some singers still include scatting in their performances, including Al Jarreau, Dave Matthews, Kurt Elling, and J.D. Walter.

Louis Armstrong was known for his wild trumpet playing, his gravelly singing voice, and his ability to scat with the best.

Even at the top of their professions, both Ella and Marilyn continued to battle stereotyping.

CHAPTER 4

An Unlikely Friendship

At first, it may be hard to understand how Ella Fitzgerald and Marilyn Monroe could be friends. In many ways, they were very different. Fitzgerald faced racism, while Monroe was adored by all. Monroe used drugs and alcohol to cope with life, while Fitzgerald refused to use either one in any way. However, underneath, the women had a lot in common—and it was those elements that brought them together.

Monroe had listened to the music of Ella Fitzgerald for years before meeting her in person. At one of Fitzgerald's performances, Monroe introduced herself. "[Marilyn] struck up a conversation with [Ella]," stated Geoffrey Mark in his book, "and what they found out was they had both been teenagers forced out on their own, they had to survive for themselves, they both had to deal with being women in a business that was completely dominated by men."[1] The two women had both had childhoods full of loneliness, struggle, and abuse. They had married young—and divorced. They had struggled to get people to see them for who they truly were: Fitzgerald because of being black was overlooked by white audiences; and Monroe, being so "blonde," was never taken seriously. The two women also shared a passion for civil rights.

Marilyn often entertained soldiers by participating in USO tours in the 1950s.

One of Monroe's foster parents delivered mail in Watts, an African American area. This helped introduce her to the black community and their continual fight for equality. Her awareness of these issues and others only increased during her marriage to Arthur Miller. In 1960, she joined the Hollywood branch of the Committee for a Sane Nuclear Policy. She once told reporters, "My nightmare is the H-bomb. What's yours?"[2] While living in Connecticut with Miller, she also was elected as an alternate delegate to the state's Democratic caucus, meaning she was certified to be a substitute when voting on state measures. In 1961, Monroe, along with movie star Shelley Winters, attended a number of rallies protesting nuclear weapons and the lack of civil rights for all.

In one of her last interviews, Monroe stated her overall philosophy: "What I really want to say, . . . that what the world needs is a real feeling of kinship. Everyone: stars, laborers, Negroes, Jews, Arabs. We are all brothers."[3] It was this attitude that led her to call Charlie Morrison to ensure that Ella Fitzgerald be allowed to perform in his nightclub.

Fitzgerald knew what it was like to be denied her equal rights from the time she was a child. Even after she had recorded hit songs and had sold out crowds, she still had to fight to get into some venues and then be allowed to come through the front door—until Marilyn Monroe stood up for her.

This photo, taken at the
Tiffany Club in 1954, is one
of the rare pictures of Ella
and Marilyn together.

Ella often closed her eyes when performing to better concentrate on the meaning of the lyrics.

In many ways Fitzgerald's determination to perform despite racial rules and laws helped advance the civil rights movement. During her lifetime, she was awarded the National Association for the Advancement of Colored People (NAACP) Equal Justice Award and the American Black Achievement Award. As the American History site states, "Fitzgerald was seen as an inspiration. Her drive pushed her career forward and by using her talent and help from friends, colleagues, and manager, she was able to break down seemingly impossible barriers."[4] In 1993, Ella established the Ella Fitzgerald Charitable Foundation to help at-risk children and to support literacy and musical education. The foundation continues today in California. She also founded the Ella Fitzgerald Child Care Center in South-Central Los Angeles.

Ella Fitzgerald and Marilyn Monroe were different in some ways, but similar in far more. Their deep belief that people were created equal and that everyone deserved the chance to shine brought them together and formed a special friendship that meant a great deal to both of them.

Meet the Ladies

If you've never seen Marilyn Monroe act or Ella Fitzgerald sing, here are the best places to start.

Marilyn's Movies	Ella's Songs
Gentlemen Prefer Blondes	"It Don't Mean a Thing"
The Seven Year Itch	"A-Tisket, A-Tasket"
How to Marry a Millionaire	"Let's Do It (Let's Fall in Love)"
Bus Stop	"Cheek to Cheek"
Some Like It Hot	"Summertime"
The Misfits	"Can't Buy Me Love"
The Prince and the Showgirl	"Someone to Watch Over Me"
Niagara	"Oh, Lady Be Good"

Despite Marilyn's bright smile, by the time she was rehearsing for *Something's Got to Give*, she was struggling daily.

CHAPTER 5

Reaching Out

Some friendships last a lifetime, while others are fleeting. Some connections last just a few weeks, months, or years. For Ella and Marilyn, their friendship had a time limit, because too soon, Marilyn would take too many pills and end her life.

During her lifetime, Marilyn was increasingly troubled by emotional and mental issues. There is evidence that mental illness is inherited, and both her grandmother and her mother had spent years in mental institutions. She was diagnosed and treated for depression several times. She saw a number of psychiatrists and had years of therapy. Although She did not leave a note before she died, her journals reveal a glimpse into her struggle. "I can't really stand human beings sometimes—I know they all have problems as I have mine—but I'm really too tired of it," she wrote. "Trying to understand, making allowances, seeing certain things that just weary me. . . . All this thought and writing has made my hands tremble but I just want to keep pouring it out until the great pot in the mind is, though not emptied, relieved." Despite these words, she also wanted to get better.

Judy Garland was a beloved singer and actress who enjoyed a long career in film and on stage. She began by potraying the character of Dorothy in the classic film *The Wizard of Oz*.

She wrote, "I can and will help myself and work on things analytically no matter how painful."[1]

No one is sure who Marilyn might have reached out to for help before she took her life. One famous actor, Judy Garland, reported that she spoke with Monroe a few months before her death. In a memoir of her life, Garland wrote, "That beautiful girl was frightened of aloneness . . . Like me she was just trying to do her job—garnish some delightful whipped cream onto some people's lives, but Marilyn and I never got a chance to talk. . . . I never saw that sweet, dear girl again. I wish I had been able to talk to her the night she died."[2]

There is no evidence that Monroe reached out to her friend Ella Fitzgerald during the last few months of her life. Certainly Fitzgerald, a woman who had known struggle all her life, might have been helpful.

Although she never had to deal with the alcohol and drug addiction that Monroe did, Fitzgerald knew what it was like to fight to be heard. For Monroe, it had been fighting against being seen as so beautiful that she could not possibly also be intelligent. For Fitzgerald, it had been the opposite. She fought to prove her talent despite not having the looks that so many other musical stars did.

Marilyn's farewell wave from the Los Angeles airport took on more importance after she died a short time later.

In one of her last interviews in the United Kingdom in early 1990, at the age of 73, Fitzgerald said, "I think that is something we should all try to be: neighbors, where we share and love each other."[3] That love for others was one of the hallmarks of her life—and one that she shared with Marilyn Monroe, the woman who once reached out to her in love and friendship.

Marilyn had Norwegian roots on her father's side. A statue of her is featured in the town of Haguesund, Norway.

Dealing with Depression

Everyone feels sad sometimes—it is just a normal part of life. However, if that sadness continues for weeks or months, or if it starts to interfere with daily life, it may be diagnosed as depression. Depression is an illness that can affect a person's sleep, concentration, and even his or her appetite. Left untreated, it can grow into feelings of guilt, hopelessness, or worthlessness.

Depression has several risk factors. It can be genetic, psychological, or social. It can also connect with other conditions, including attention deficit hyperactivity disorder (ADHD), eating disorders, obsessive compulsive disorder (OCD), or addiction. If you or a friend is experiencing any of these feelings, or you feel like you need help, please reach out to your family, friends, or teachers. You can also contact one of many 24-hour, toll-free hotlines, including the following:

National Suicide Prevention Lifeline	800-273-8255
National Alliance on Mental Illness Helpline	800-950-6264
The Trevor Lifeline (LGBTQ)	866-488-7386
LGBT National Hotline	888-843-4564

More hotlines and helpful resources are available at Teen Health and Wellness, https://teenhealthandwellness.com/static/hotlines.

1917   Ella Fitzgerald is born on April 25.

1926   Marilyn Monroe is born Norma Jean Mortenson on June 1. She was baptized as Norma Jean (or Jeane) Baker.

1934   Ella appears in Amateur Night at the Apollo and is signed to a recording contract with Chick Webb.

1935   Ella records her first song, "Love and Kisses."

1941   The Mocambo opens in West Hollywood, California. Ella marries Benjamin Kornegay.

1942   Marilyn marries Johnny Dougherty.

1944   Norman Granz starts a concert series called Jazz at the Philharmonic.

1946   Marilyn divorces Dougherty and signs her first movie contract.

1947   Ella marries Ray Brown.

1949   Marilyn has her first movie role in *Love Happy*.

1950   Marilyn appears in *The Asphalt Jungle*.

1953   Ella divorces Brown.

1954   Marilyn marries Joe DiMaggio; they divorce later that year.

1956   Marilyn marries Arthur Miller.

1961   Marilyn divorces Miller and films her last movie, *The Misfits*. With Shelley Winters, she attends rallies protesting nuclear weapons.

1962   Marilyn sings "Happy Birthday" to President John F. Kennedy. In August, at the age of 36, she dies of a drug overdose.

1965   Ella almost collapses on stage in Munich.

1967   Ella is awarded the Lifetime Achievement Award.

1972   Ella and Carol Channing perform in the half-time show at Super Bowl VI.

1986   Ella has quintuple bypass heart surgery.

1987   Ella is awarded the National Medal of Arts.

1991   At Carnegie Hall, Ella gives her last concert.

1993   Ella's lower legs are amputated. She establishes the Ella Fitzgerald Charitable Foundation.

1996   In June, at age 79, Ella dies.

Ella Fitzgerald in concert, 1968

Chapter 1

1. Saunders, Clarissa. "Marilyn and Ella: The 'Truth' behind Ella's Booking at the Mocambo." *Stars and Letters*, May 8, 2018. https://starsandletters. blogspot.com/2018/05/marilyn-ella-truth-behind-ellas-booking.html

2. Nolasco, Stephanie. "Ella Fitzgerald and Marilyn Monroe Bonded after Suffering from Abusive Childhoods, Book Claims." *Fox News*, April 2, 2018. https://www.foxnews.com/entertainment/ ella-fitzgerald-and-marilyn-monroe-bonded-after-suffering-from- abusive-childhoods-book-claims

Chapter 2

1. Rothman, Lily. "Marilyn Monroe's Forgotten Radical Politics." *Time*, June 1, 2016. http://time.com/4346542/radical-politics-marilyn-monroe/

2. Steinem, Gloria. "The Woman Who Will Not Die." PBS, *American Masters*,1986.

3. Byrne, Ciar. "Marilyn and Ella: The Meeting of the Misfits." *The Independent*, February 13, 2008.

Chapter 3

1. Holden, Stephen. "Ella Fitzgerald, the Voice of Jazz, Dies at 79." *The New York Times*, June 16, 1996.

2. Nolasco, Stephanie. "Ella Fitzgerald and Marilyn Monroe Bonded after Suffering from Abusive Childhoods, Book Claims." *Fox News*, April 2, 2018.

3. Ibid.

4. Holden.

5. Ibid.

6. PBS, "Something to Live For." *American Masters*. June 1, 2005

7. Holden.

Chapter 4

1. Nolasco, Stephanie. "Ella Fitzgerald and Marilyn Monroe Bonded after Suffering from Abusive Childhoods, Book Claims." *Fox News*, April 2,

2. Kettler, Sara. "Marilyn Monroe: Fascinating Facts about the Real Woman Behind the Legend." *Biography*, August 3, 2017.
3. Steinem, Gloria, and George Barris. *Marilyn: Norma Jeane*. New York: New American Library, 1988.
4. Kuske, Rebecca. "Ella Fitzgerald: Breaking Down Racial Barriers with Her Voice." *Smithsonian*, April 1, 2017.

Chapter 5

1. Dixon, Christine-Marie Liwag. "Shocking Things We Learned about Marilyn Monroe After Her Death." *The List*, Undated. https://www.thelist.com/78083/shocking-things-learned-marilyn-monroe-death/
2. McNeil, Liz. "Judy Garland's Shocking Revelation about Marilyn Monroe: 'She Asked Me for Help.' " *People*, January 26, 2017.
3. YouTube. "Ella Fitzgerald on Aspel: 3 March 1990: Part 2."

Marilyn Monroe visiting troops on a USO tour.

Books

Hansen, Grace. *Ella Fitzgerald: American Jazz Singer*. Minneapolis, Minnesota: ABDO Kids, 2016.

Ollivier, Stephanie. *Ella Fitzgerald (First Discovery Music)*. United Kingdom: Moonlight Publishing, 2016.

Small, Cathleen. *American Life and Celebrity Icons from Marilyn Monroe to Taylor Swift*. New York: Cavendish Square, 2016.

Works Consulted

"1941: Mocambo Opens." Playground to the Stars. © 2010–2019. http://www.playgroundtothestars.com/timeline/1941-mocambo-opens/

Bernstein, Nina. "Ward of the State; The Gap in Ella Fitzgerald's Life." *The New York Times*. June 23, 1996. https://www.nytimes.com/1996/06/23/weekinreview/ward-of-the-state-the-gap-in-ella-fitzgerald-s-life.html

Burrows, George. "How Scat Singing Became an Expressive Language in Its Own Right." *The Independent*. October 29, 2018. https://www.independent.co.uk/arts-entertainment/music/features/scat-singing-definition-jazz-history-louis-armstrong-ella-fitzgerald-cab-calloway-slavery-african-a8607061.html

Corliss, Richard. "Marilyn Monroe 50 Years Later: In TIME and Out of Time." *Time*. August 3, 2012. http://entertainment.time.com/2012/08/03/marilyn-monroe-50-years-later-in-time-and-out-of-time/

Dixon, Christine-Marie Liwag. "Shocking Things We Learned about Marilyn Monroe after Her Death." *The List*. Undated. https://www.thelist.com/78083/shocking-things-learned-marilyn-monroe-death/

"Ella Fitzgerald." United States History. Undated. https://www.u-s-history.com/pages/h3868.html

"Ella Fitzgerald on Aspel: 3 March 1990: Part 2." https://www.youtube.com/watch?v=DFDJ4PiXm2E

Holden, Stephen. "Ella Fitzgerald, the Voice of Jazz, Dies at 79." *The New York Times,* June 16, 1996. https://www.nytimes.com/1996/06/16/nyregion/ella-fitzgerald-the-voice-of-jazz-dies-at-79.html

Kettler, Sara. "Marilyn Monroe: Fascinating Facts about the Real Woman Behind the Legend." *Biography.* August 3, 2017. https://www.biography.com/news/marilyn-monroe-biography-facts

Kniestedt. Kevin. "How Marilyn Monroe Changed Ella Fitzgerald's Life." *KNKX.* March 22, 2012. https://www.knkx.org/post/how-marilyn-monroe-changed-ella-fitzgeralds-life

Kuske, Rebecca. "Ella Fitzgerald: Breaking Down Racial Barriers with Her Voice." *Smithsonian.* April 1, 2017. http://americanhistory.si.edu/blog/ella-fitzgerald-voice

"Marilyn and Ella: The Meeting of the Misfits." *Independent.* February 13, 2008. https://www.independent.co.uk/arts-entertainment/theatre-dance/features/marilyn-and-ella-the-meeting-of-the-misfits-781442.html

Marilyn Monroe Collection. "Marilyn Monroe Biography." © 2019. http://themarilynmonroecollection.com/marilyn-monroe/

McNeil, Liz. "Judy Garland's Shocking Revelation about Marilyn Monroe: 'She Asked Me for Help.'" *People.* January 26, 2017. https://people.com/books/judy-garlands-shocking-revelation-about-marilyn-monroe-she-asked-me-for-help/

Nolasco, Stephanie. "Ella Fitzgerald and Marilyn Monroe Bonded after Suffering from Abusive Childhoods, Book Claims." *Fox News.* April 2, 2018. https://www.foxnews.com/entertainment/ella-fitzgerald-and-marilyn-monroe-bonded-after-suffering-from-abusive-childhoods-book-claims

PBS: "Something to Live For." *American Masters*. June 1, 2005. http://www.pbs.org/wnet/americanmasters/ella-fitzgerald-something-to-live-for/590/

Rothman, Lily. "Marilyn Monroe's Forgotten Radical Politics." *Time*. June 1, 2016. http://time.com/4346542/radical-politics-marilyn-monroe/

Saunders, Clarissa. "Marilyn and Ella: The 'Truth' behind Ella's Booking at the Mocambo." *Stars and Letters*, May 8, 2018. https://starsandletters.blogspot.com/2018/05/marilyn-ella-truth-behind-ellas-booking.html

Steinem, Gloria. "The Woman Who Will Not Die." *American Masters*, 1986. http://www.pbs.org/wnet/americanmasters/marilyn-monroe-biography/61/

Steinem, Gloria, and George Barris. *Marilyn: Norma Jeane*. New York: New American Library, 1988. http://time.com/4346542/radical-politics-marilyn-monroe/

On the Internet

Kiddle: Ella Fitzgerald
https://kids.kiddle.co/Ella_Fitzgerald

KidsKonnect: Ella Fitzgerald
https://kidskonnect.com/people/ella-fitzgerald/

Kiddle: Marilyn Monroe
https://kids.kiddle.co/Marilyn_Monroe

KidsKonnect: Marilyn Monroe
https://kidskonnect.com/people/marilyn-monroe/

accommodations (uh-KAH-muh-DAY-shuns)—Rooms, food, and other services for travelers, such as one would find at a hotel.

amputate (AM-pyoo-tayt)—To surgically remove from the body.

annul (uh-NUL)—To declare a marriage invalid.

be-bop (BEE-bop)—A type of very fast jazz music.

documentary (dok-yoo-MEN-tuh-ree)—A factual television show or movie.

H-bomb (AITCH-bomb)—Short for "hydrogen bomb," a powerful nuclear weapon.

immigrant (IH-mih-grent)—A person who moves into a country from somewhere else.

improvise (IM-proh-vyz)—To make up on the spot.

Merchant Marine (MUR-chint mah-REEN)—A sailor who serves on a country's fleet of commercial ships.

miscarriage (MIS-kayr-idj)—To lose a baby before it comes to term.

munition (myoo-NIH-shuns)—Military supplies.

playwright (PLAY-ryt)—A person who writes plays.

reformatory (reh-FOR-muh-tor-ee)—An institution for young people who have committed crimes.

scat (SKAT)—A style of singing with nonsense words.

stereotyping (STAYR-ee-oh-ty-ping)—To use a simple, general idea about a person based on their looks, religion, background, or other trait instead of the person's true character.

USO (United Service Organization)—The group that provides entertainment for active military personnel.